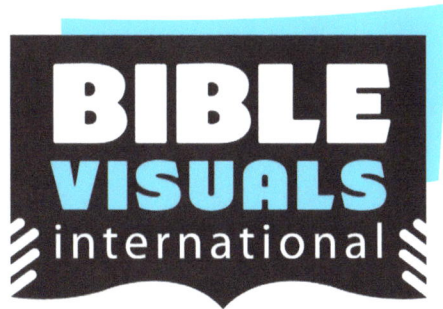

BIBLE VISUALS international

Helping Children See Jesus

ISBN: 978-1-64104-104-1

Fanny Crosby
The Blind Poet

Authors: Doris Stuber Moose, Karen E. Weitzel
Illustrator: Vernon Henkel
Computer Graphic Artists: Ed Olson, Melody Mayer
Page Layout: Patricia Pope, Charity Taft

© 2020 Bible Visuals International
PO Box 153, Akron, PA 17501-0153
Phone: (717) 859-1131
www.biblevisuals.org

RELATED ITEMS

To access related items (such as activities, memory verse posters and translated texts) please visit our web store at shop.biblevisuals.org and enter 5130 in the search box on the page.

FREE TEXT DOWNLOAD

To access a FREE printable copy of the teaching text (PDF format) in English or other available languages, enter S5130DL in the search box. Add the item to your cart, and use coupon code XTACSV17 at checkout. Once your order is processed you will receive an email with a link to the free download.

- 15 -

For we walk
by faith,
not by
sight....

2 Corinthians 5:7

Chapter 1

NOTE TO THE TEACHER

One of Fanny Crosby's songs, "To God Be the Glory", is available from the publisher of this volume. This is a song of praise which glorifies God for the redemption He has provided through His Son. A suggestion for introducing this song is found on page 14 under "Making Music."

The *aim* of the chapter: To discover that God sometimes allows us to go through difficult circumstances we don't understand, but He can use them for our good.

Brush, one ... brush, two ... brush, three ... brush, four ... brush, five ... brushing and counting at the same time kept four-year-old Fanny busy for a while. And, Grandmother was glad. Brush, six ... brush, sev .... The brush slipped out of the little girl's hand and clattered to the floor.

Fanny got down on her knees and felt the floor around her. "Grandma, where's my hairbrush?"

Grandmother left her rocker, picked up the brush and placed it in Fanny's hand. "Here, Fanny. Now, start again," she said, as she guided the child's hand.

Show Illustration #1

Fanny was tired of brushing. She wanted to talk. "Grandma, why can't I see?" It was a question she had often asked before, and a question Grandmother had often answered.

"Fanny, you could see at one time, but only when you were a tiny baby," Grandmother replied. "I've told you before what happened to your eyes."

"But I want to hear again, Grandma," Fanny interrupted. She leaned against Grandmother's rocking chair waiting for the story she knew would come.

"It was a cold March night when you were born right here in this cottage." Grandmother knew Fanny enjoyed hearing about the storm, so she always made it fierce. "The wind swirled around our house. It rattled the windows and squeezed through the cracks. We wrapped you snugly in a blanket and your mother held you close. Guess who wanted to hold you the next day?"

Since Fanny knew the story almost well enough to tell it herself, she said, "It was Polly!"

"Yes," Grandmother said, "it was Polly. She was only three years old, but she wanted to hold you. When I placed you in her arms, she asked, 'Can I play with her?'"

Fanny laughed. "I play with Polly now," she said, "when she's not in school."

Polly was Grandmother's daughter, and so she was Fanny's aunt, even though she was not much older than Fanny.

Grandmother continued her story. "Your father always rocked you in this chair at night. It was hard plowing the rocky ground in our fields and he was so tired. But he was not too tired to play with you. He and your mother played a game. They wiggled their fingers in front of your face until your eyes followed them.

"When you were six weeks old, you became sick with a cold. Your eyes turned red and sore. And you cried loudly and waved your tiny fists. We tried to find the doctor, but he was away. Another man, who said he was a doctor, came to treat you. We watched this man put hot cloths over your eyes. He said they would draw out the infection and wouldn't hurt you."

"Did I cry, Grandma?"

"Yes, Fanny, you cried. After the treatment, you improved every day. But white scars covered your eyes. The hot cloths had injured them."

"I couldn't play Daddy and Mamma's game anymore 'cause I couldn't see their fingers," Fanny stated. "But I can play other games now without seeing. I'm going outside to wait for Polly."

Fanny had learned her way around the house and yard by touching every object she bumped into as she walked. Over and over she had practiced and memorized where everything was located. Now she confidently skipped across the room and stood in the open doorway. With a hop she landed on the doorstep. And then she was running toward the stone fence.

The little girl was learning to climb those stone fences. They divided all the farms in the southeast corner of New York State where she lived. And Polly had been teaching her how to scramble up into the maple trees in the woods behind their home.

"I hear you, woodpecker," Fanny called as she hauled up her long skirt and pulled herself onto a large rock. This was her best-liked spot from which to play a game of pretend.

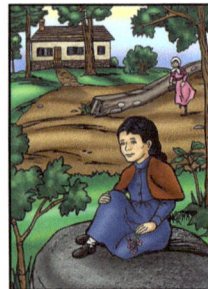

Show Illustration #2

Tap-tap-tap. *That woodpecker's in the big oak tree in the woods*, she thought listening to the sharp sounds. *Grandma said she saw his hole there. When Polly comes, we'll walk in the woods and find it. And we can pick violets, too. I'll give mine to Mother when she comes home.*

Fanny clapped her hands against the rock. It felt warm today. She lifted her head. She could tell the difference between light and dark. The sky was bright so that meant the sun was shining. Maybe she would even be able to see the bright red glow in the sunset tonight. But that would be all she could see. After that everything would become dark because it was nighttime. Not even hundreds of candles would help her to see as Polly could.

Fanny swung around on the rock and faced the woods. The wind was whistling through the trees. Grandmother said it sounded like the ocean. Today Fanny pretended she was a sailor. There was a terrible storm and she was standing at the masthead of a large ship. She jumped up and felt the wind blowing her hair across her face.

I can't really be a sailor when I'm grown up, Fanny thought and then giggled as she sat down. *Girls can't be sailors. I want to go to school as Polly does. Then I can be someone special.*

A dog barked. And Fanny heard the sound of running footsteps. She twisted around. "Is that you, Polly?"

"Yes, Fanny. I'm coming," Polly called as she ran up the dirt road.

Fanny slid off the stone. "Someday I'll go to school with you, Polly. Then we can come home together."

Polly was silent. Then, "Maybe, Fanny," she said slowly. "But how will you read your lessons? You can't learn unless you can read. And you can't read because you can't see."

"But I can learn if someone helps me." Fanny sounded determined. "Grandma helped me learn to dress myself and to brush my hair . . .and to eat without spilling food . . . and to learn where all the furniture is. I can walk–and run–and not bump into anything. And I can hear sounds you can't."

Polly hugged the little girl. "You're smart, Fanny. You can tell what tree a leaf came from just by feeling it. And you know all the birds and their songs."

"I heard the woodpecker today. Let's go to the woods and find his tree," Fanny begged as she pulled the older girl's hand.

They didn't see Grandmother standing in the doorway of the one-story home watching them cross the field and enter the woods. "Lord," Grandmother whispered, "I will do my best to teach Fanny if You will give me the wisdom, patience and strength." Then she went inside to prepare supper.

Show Illustration #1

It was nearly bedtime. Fanny put her head against Grandmother's shoulder. The slow rocking was making her sleepy. Grandmother had said the chapter she was reading from the Bible was her favorite. What was she reading now?

". . . a God of truth and without iniquity …"

"Grandma, what's 'niquity?" Fanny asked standing up straight beside Grandmother.

"Iniquity is another word for sin. Sin is doing wrong. God in Heaven never does wrong, Fanny. He is a God who always does what is right," Grandmother explained.

"God has never sinned and He never will," Grandmother continued. "But you and I have sinned. When you do wrong, your mother or I punish you. God, too, punishes us for our wrong. The punishment for sin is death. But God is so kind and loving. He sent His only Son Jesus Christ to earth. Jesus was punished for our sin instead of us. He died on the cross and three days later came alive. He became the Saviour of the world. He wants you to know and love Him."

Fanny listened carefully, although she didn't understand all that Grandmother was telling her.

Grandmother rocked a while without speaking. "Fanny, God has something special planned for you." Then softly she hummed a hymn.

Fanny rubbed her fingers over the worn, smooth arm of the rocking chair. *Maybe I can go to school. That's special.* "Let's pray." Grandmother's voice urged Fanny to slip down beside the rocking chair and bury her face in Grandma's lap.

Show Illustration #3

Later that evening Mercy Crosby looked down at her daughter Fanny curled up in bed. "If only she could see," she sighed brushing the tears from her cheeks. "What will become of her? She will never see the flowers she loves to smell. She will never read a book . . . though, maybe she will–if my plan works."

Fanny's mother stumbled to her cot, weary from serving as a maid all day. Since her husband died, she had worked for a wealthy family nearby. Now there was almost enough money saved. Soon Mercy could tell little Fanny of her plan.

Grandmother, seeing Mercy's tears, pointed to the table as she spoke, "Fanny picked those violets for you today."

"Oh, Mother," Mercy cried, "I wish Fanny could see them."

Grandmother put her hand gently on Mercy's arm. "What can't be cured, can be endured, daughter. Sometimes God allows what we cannot understand. Perhaps later on we'll learn why He's allowed Fanny to be blind."

Mercy sat on her cot and stared into the darkness of the room. The candle flickered on the table as a gust of wind blew in the window. "No!" she said firmly. "Fanny will see!" Into the night Mercy sat planning what she would tell Fanny one day.

The months went by, Mercy kept thinking about her plan. Finally, the day came when she had saved enough money. "Fanny, come here," she called.

Fanny walked slowly toward the house. She didn't want to leave Polly and her friends in the middle of their game. But Mother had called. Fanny knew by Mother's voice she had better obey.

She wrinkled her forehead as she tried to think what she did wrong that afternoon. She hadn't torn her dress again, though she felt her skirt just to make sure. Brushing her black curls out of her face, she pushed open the door.

Squeak, squeak, squeak. Hearing that, Fanny knew Mother was in Grandma's rocking chair.

It was time for Mercy to tell Fanny of her plan. "Fanny," she began as she stopped rocking, "tomorrow we are going to travel to a big city. We shall ride in a wagon to the river. We'll get in a sailboat there and sail down the river for many miles to New York City."

Fanny clapped her hands as she hopped in circles. A trip with Mother! And to a big city. She suddenly stood still. "Why are we going, Mamma?"

"We are going to see a famous doctor, Fanny," Mercy said slowly. "He's going to look at your eyes. And…. if he can, he might operate, that is, make your eyes so they can see."

Mercy continued quickly, "The operation will hurt a little, but afterwards you might see. When we come home, you can look at Polly's picture books."

Five-year-old Fanny ran outside to tell Polly. "Polly!" She shrieked. "Polly! Mamma said I might see your picture books. We're gonna see a doctor. He might make my eyes see." Fanny grabbed Polly's hands, hopping and pulling her in circles. She forgot that the doctor would have to hurt her eyes so she could see.

Show Illustration #4

Several days later Fanny sat in the doctor's office. She held her mother's hand tightly. Dr. Mott and another eye specialist examined her eyes.

"Fanny," Dr. Mott asked quietly as he placed his hand on her head, "Would you like me to fix your eyes so you can see?"

What would Fanny say? Would the doctor be able to fix her eyes? We'll find out in the next chapter!

The aim of the chapter: To learn to listen and respond to God when He speaks to our hearts about sin.

Fanny had taken a trip to New York City with her mother to see if the famous Dr. Mott could operate on Fanny's eyes. But when Dr. Mott asked Fanny if she wanted him to fix her eyes, she wasn't sure.

The little girl pulled away and reached for her mother. Hadn't Mother said it would hurt? Suddenly she was afraid. "No, Sir," Fanny replied timidly. She listened as the man told Mercy that Fanny could see light and bright colors, but nothing else. The scars on her eyes could not be removed.

"Poor child," Dr. Mott said kindly, "I'm afraid you will never see."

Mercy covered her face with her hands and wept bitterly. "Don't cry, Mamma," Fanny whispered. She hugged her mother. "Let's go home," she said.

Fanny was eager for the boat ride home. She liked hearing the waves slap against the boat. The cool river breezes blew her hair in every direction. And the captain told her exciting stories about the sea.

But Mercy was quiet and sad. Fanny thought, *I can't see and Mamma wants me to.* She tapped her feet on the deck and watched the reds and oranges in the sky. Hour after hour as the waves lapped the boat they seemed to say, "Fanny, be brave. Fanny, be brave. Happier days are coming."

One evening Fanny knelt to pray by Grandma's chair. In a puzzled voice she asked, "Why didn't God answer Mamma's prayer so I could see?"

Grandma stroked Fanny's hair as she answered. "God can do anything, child. He gives us what is best. We must never want anything that does not agree with His plan for us. God has something special for you to do, Fanny, even though you cannot see."

Shortly after the visit to New York, Mercy went to work for another family. Fanny and her mother had to move. Fanny missed Grandmother, the woods and horseback rides in the fields with Polly. But Grandmother traveled the six miles to see her several times a week. And Fanny often went back to visit Grandmother.

Show Illustration #1

Now that Fanny was older, Grandma read more of the Bible to her. Each week she memorized parts Grandmother assigned. She learned quickly.

When Fanny was eight years old, one day she said, "Grandma, I wrote a poem this week. I want you to hear it.

Oh, what a happy child I am,
Although I cannot see!
I am resolved that in this world
Contented I will be!
How many blessings I enjoy
That other people don't!
To weep or sigh because I'm blind,
I cannot and I won't."

"That's wonderful, Fanny," Grandmother said. Fanny could hear she was pleased. "God has given you a good mind. Learn to use it for Him."

Then Fanny and Mercy had to move a second time. This time it was farther away. While Mercy worked as a housekeeper for a wealthy family, Fanny stayed with their landlady.

Mrs. Hawley often took her into the garden. Fanny enjoyed naming the flowers as she felt each one.

"Mrs. Hawley, I smell roses," Fanny exclaimed one day.

"Yes, Fanny. Come, I'll show you my prize white roses. Then I'll listen to you say the chapters of the Bible you've learned."

Fanny reached out to touch the soft petals. "Ouch! I'm glad all flowers don't have thorns," she said as she rubbed her finger.

"I hope those thorns will keep people from cutting down my roses," Mrs. Hawley replied. "I prize these roses more than my other flowers."

After going into the house Mrs. Hawley sat in a chair, her much-read Bible and a book of poetry on her lap. Fanny stood before her and recited five chapters from Genesis she had memorized that week. Then, just as Grandmother had done, Mrs. Hawley read and explained four more chapters. By the end of the first year, Fanny knew all of Genesis, Exodus, Leviticus and Numbers, as well as Matthew, Mark, Luke and John.

Show Illustration #5

Often Fanny sat alone thinking of the poems Mrs. Hawley had read or the Bible chapters she was to memorize. When Fanny heard the laughing voices of children returning home from school, she sighed wistfully *Will I ever learn like other children?* She had gone to school several times. But the school teacher did not have time to teach her, so Fanny stayed home.

More determined than ever, she memorized all she heard. *I'll show everyone what a blind girl can do,* she thought. In Sunday school contests Fanny quoted the longest and most difficult verses she knew. And she always won the prize!

One afternoon, Mrs. Hawley called Fanny to her. "One of my white roses has been cut. Did you break off the flower?" she asked quietly.

"Oh, no, Mrs. Hawley," Fanny replied quickly.

"I suppose someone has been in the yard and helped himself to my flowers. Very well, you may go play. I'll keep asking until I find who took the rose."

Fanny climbed the stairs to her room and sat by the window. *I hope she doesn't find out,* Fanny worried. *I shouldn't have lied. Mrs. Hawley will be unhappy with me if she discovers I cut the rose.* Instead of joining the neighbor children whom she heard outdoors, Fanny sat by herself. What would Mrs. Hawley do to her? Her stomach felt strange.

Show Illustration #6

Later in the day her landlady called upstairs, "Fanny, we haven't read today. I have a story for you." Fanny listened as the older woman read of Ananias and

Sapphira who were struck dead for lying to the Holy Spirit. Her chest felt tight when Mrs. Hawley said, "Fanny, I saw you cut that rose this morning. I'm disappointed that you lied to me. God is displeased, too."

"Oh, Mrs. Hawley, I'm sorry. I'll never tell a lie again," Fanny cried.

"I forgive you, Fanny," Mrs. Hawley said gently to the weeping girl. "God, too, forgives us when we confess our wrong to Him. I hope you will always remember that. And I hope you will never lie to me again."

As the months passed, Mercy noticed Fanny was often sad. She knew her young daughter, soon to be 12, was frustrated because she could not go to school. Mercy was amazed at the poems Fanny wrote. How she wished her daughter could go to school.

One night, during a visit with her grandmother, Fanny mentioned again her desire to learn.

As Grandmother always did when there was a problem, she knelt with Fanny by the old rocking chair and prayed aloud.

After Grandmother left, Fanny felt her way over to the open window. Through her scarred eyes she could see a faint light–the moon was shining. Quietly she prayed, "Dear God, please show me how I can learn and be like other children." The sadness Fanny had felt slowly went away. She did not know how she would learn, but she knew God would answer in His own time.

When Fanny next visited, Grandmother was ill. "God is going to call me away soon," she told the child. She hushed Fanny's sobbing to whisper a question. "Will you meet me in Heaven someday?"

There was a pause, then Fanny answered with a knot in her throat, "By the grace of God, I will, Grandma." But Fanny only said this to comfort her Grandmother. She'd never come to God as a sinner and believed on His Son. As Grandmother hugged Fanny she said, "Keep memorizing God's Word, Fanny. He'll show you His plan. God does have something special for you."

One fall afternoon when Fanny was fourteen, she heard the crackle of dried leaves and quick snapping of twigs as someone approached her.

"Fanny," her mother's breathless voice exclaimed, "listen to this!"

Show Illustration #7

The rustle of paper in Mercy's hand and the seriousness of her voice frightened Fanny. *Someone is sick or has died*, she thought. But her fright was soon gone as Mercy explained, "Fanny, there is a school called the New York Institute for the Blind. This paper tells all about it. Would you like to go there?"

Fanny clasped her hands tightly. A tingle of excitement raced through her. School! A chance to learn and be like other people. *Oh, thank You, God!* Fanny prayed silently. *You have answered my prayer.*

The young girl trembled as she spoke. "Yes, Mother. Yes, I do want to go. This is the happiest day of my life!"

Fanny applied to the school and was accepted. The next four months were busy as she prepared to leave. Often there was sadness in Mercy's voice as the two talked. "How will you ever get along without me? You've never been away from home more than two weeks at a time!"

Fanny answered thoughtfully, "I love you, Mother. And I'll miss you. But I want to be like my friends. I want an education."

On the morning Fanny was to leave, her mother wakened her at the last minute. Fanny shook as she dressed quickly. By the time she was ready the stagecoach was waiting. There was a knot in her throat as she tried to swallow her breakfast. Tears were in her eyes as she climbed into the stage. She couldn't speak.

The stagecoach bumped its way over the rough road. Fanny and the woman who was taking her to school bounced on the seats. With every bounce, a tear trickled down Fanny's cheek. After an hour, Fanny's companion said, "If you don't want to go to New York City, we'll get out at the next station and take the returning stage home. Your mother will be lonesome without you anyway."

Fanny's lip quivered. Something in her wanted to say, *Yes, please take me home!* The thought startled her. Not go to school? "No," Fanny said firmly, "I shall go to New York and school."

The first evening at school Fanny sat in a little room that was to be hers. Everything was new and strange. The furniture was arranged differently from home. *I'll have to learn how to walk around without bumping into the bed and chair*, she thought as she sat on her trunk. Tears filled her eyes again. But then she reasoned, *I'm at school. I'm going to learn. I'll meet new friends.* Over and over Fanny tried to think pleasant thoughts.

She didn't realize how much her sigh sounded like a sob until a kindly Quaker woman put her arms around her. "Fanny, I think thee has never been away from home before." The words sounded a bit strange, but the voice was kind.

"No, Ma'am," Fanny replied meekly. "Please excuse me. I must cry." And she did.

Fanny soon adjusted to school life. Her new friends explained the schedule and showed her around. "Remember. If you're late for morning prayers," one cautioned, "no breakfast for you!" Fanny laughed, eager to begin classes.

Several weeks later, Fanny sent a letter home. (*Teacher:* Before the class begins, print the following letters on two sheets of paper and place in two envelopes. Remove and read aloud where indicated. Read letter #1 from envelope.)

"Dear Mother, Thank you for allowing me to come to the Institute for the Blind. School is all I hoped it would be. When I arrived, so much was strange. I missed you–and still do! But now I've made friends.

"Classes are not so difficult when I memorize all my lessons. But when I have to read them in Braille it takes so long. It's easier to memorize than read Braille. My fingers are too calloused from playing the guitar and knitting. They aren't sensitive enough to feel the little bumps that cover the pages of our books. Those bumps are supposed to spell out words.

"I like all my classes, especially astronomy. I remember Grandma describing the stars as 'tiny, bright twinkly lights in the black sky' and that God in Heaven made them for us to enjoy. There's one class I hate and that is mathematics. Numbers frustrate me!"

Many letters later, Mercy opened another envelope and read:

(*Teacher:* Read letter from second envelope.)

"Every evening different teachers read poems and stories by famous authors. Some of my friends are trying to write and I am as well. They say I'm talented. Here are some poems I've written. I'm trying to make my poems sound like those I've heard."

One day Fanny slipped into a friend's room and quietly closed the door. "Jean," she whispered. "I just heard the gardener say the watermelon crop is to be sold. That means no more watermelons to eat. I have an idea."

The two girls walked slowly over the school grounds toward the garden.

Show Illustration #8

"Hey, now, what do you girls think you're doing out here?" growled the old gardener. "I've work to do–no time for talking. Got to load these melons in this wagon."

Thump! Bump, bump. One melon landed in the wagon and rolled. Thump.

"Sir," Fanny said, stepping forward. "We heard you are going to sell these watermelons to raise money for the school."

"Yes, yes," panted the old man. "Only a few more to load and my job's finished, except for seeing to it no one steals any."

"Let us help you," Fanny volunteered.

"You! No, Ma'am. Lifting melons is a man's job."

"Oh, I didn't mean that," Fanny said quickly. "We can guard the melons and you can rest."

"Wel-l-l . . ." the gardener drawled. "Seems I could rest a bit. You guard these melons and don't let anyone come and take one. You hear?"

"Yes, Sir," Fanny replied.

The girls waited as the gardener trudged away. Soon they heard only the chatter of a squirrel in a nearby tree. Fanny walked around to the back of the wagon and reached over the gate.

"Jean, come stand by me. The gardener said we weren't to let anyone come take a melon, but he didn't say we couldn't. Help me lift this one from the wagon. We can hide it in the lilac bushes by the path and pick it up later."

Soon the girls were sitting under a tree listening for the gardener's return. Jean giggled. "Fanny, are you going to write a poem about stealing the watermelon?"

Fanny laughed nervously. "I don't know. At least I won't write about it right away. Let's enjoy eating it first."

Jean's question had startled Fanny. Suddenly she remembered memorizing the Bible with Grandmother. She seemed to hear Grandmother's strong voice saying over and over, "Thou shalt not steal . . . thou shalt not steal." God was speaking to Fanny's heart through His Word, but she would not listen.

"I wish I could write poetry like you," Jean sighed. "Someday you're going to be famous. You wrote the words to the march we sang the other week. And you're only 17! Imagine! We sang *your* song in front of the mayor of New York City!"

Fanny had been at the Institute for a while when her teachers noticed something about her which disturbed them. She had become quite popular with both students and teachers. She had learned to play the piano, organ and harp. She was well liked wherever she went. She often received compliments on her poetry and Fanny herself was beginning to think her poetry was quite good.

Show Illustration #9

One morning after breakfast, Dr. Jones, the Institute's superintendent, called her into his office. Fanny thought to herself as she entered the room, *He wants to ask me to write a poem for some occasion or commend me for something good I have done.*

Fanny smiled to herself. But is that really what Dr. Jones wanted to talk to her about? We'll find out in the next chapter!

Chapter 3

The *aim* of the chapter: To see that the most important person we need to meet and follow is Jesus Christ, the Son of God.

Fanny had been called to talk to Dr. Jones, the superintendent of the school for the blind. She was sure he would ask her to write a special poem or tell her what a good job she was doing.

Instead, she heard these surprising words, "Fanny, I am sorry you have believed what others have said about your poems. You know very little about poetry.

"Do not spend so much time thinking up poems and waiting for people to praise you. Seek to please God first by becoming what He wants you to be."

Fanny was shocked and hurt. Hot tears spilled over onto her cheeks. It would have been easy to be angry. But something inside her said, "He tells the truth, Fanny, and it is for your own good."

Her voice trembled, "Dr. Jones, you have talked to me as my father would have talked were he living. Thank you. Forgive me for being proud of what I've done."

Soon Fanny began helping others by tutoring students. The students learned and Fanny discovered she could teach. *I shall become a teacher*, she decided. Still she continued writing poems, one after the other.

Again Fanny was called to Dr. Jones's office. He was afraid she was writing poems to escape her other work. In a solemn voice he announced, "You are to write no poetry for three months."

Three months! Fanny couldn't believe it. Words floated around in her head as she tried to study. Words she wanted to put into poems but she wasn't allowed to do so. Rhymes filled her mind when she tried to recite in class. She couldn't concentrate. She couldn't study. She failed in class. *I can't stand this*, Fanny cried to herself. *But I must obey. How shall I ever get through these three months?*

Fanny tried to study, but she just couldn't. Everything in her mind was so mixed up.

Knock. Knock. Knock.

"Come in," Fanny called.

"Dr. Jones wants to see you in his office," a student told Fanny.

Fanny's heart pounded as she left her room.

Show Illustration #9

For the third time Fanny stood in his office. *What is he going to say?* she worried. *It's been six weeks since I've written a poem.*

"Fanny, the teachers tell me your grades are slipping. Why is this?"

Truthfully she answered, "I think of poems constantly. I've tried not to, but I can't help it."

Dr. Jones tapped his pen against the desk. "Can you get good grades and pay attention in class if you are allowed to write poetry again?"

"Oh, yes, Sir. I know I can!" she answered with assurance.

The no-poetry rule was lifted. And Fanny was encouraged to write.

Dr. Jones now was determined she should develop this talent. He found a private teacher who was kind but strict. Sometimes the teacher said, "Fanny, you've not written your verses yet. It is fifteen minutes until lunchtime. If the poem isn't written by then, no lunch." Fanny wrote the poem! Soon she could take long, difficult poems and rewrite them in simpler language.

People began calling Fanny the "Blind Poetess." The US government gave money to help support the New York Institute for the Blind so government officials often toured the school. Fanny became their most popular guide because she could compose and recite poems about anyone who visited the school.

Once the superintendent rushed into her room. "The president of the United States is here. Will you compose a poem?"

Fanny's heart skipped a beat. "The president! I'm going to meet the president?" Fanny questioned excitedly. *What shall I say?* she thought. *How can I honor him?* Ten minutes later she was introduced to President Tyler. Calmly she quoted her new poem.

Returning to her room she said to herself, *I wish I could spend more time with these important men. There is so much I could learn from them.* As she sat down and picked up her knitting, she had an idea. She didn't have to wait long to try it!

The governor of New York came to visit. Fanny entered one of the rooms through which the visitors would pass. Sitting down she began to knit. Muffled voices and footsteps grew louder and then the door was thrown open. The group entered the room.

Show Illustration #10

"Governor, this is Miss Fanny Crosby, one of our students," the superintendent said proudly.

"Miss Crosby," the governor began, "I'm very pleased to meet you. I've heard of your poems–and read some, too. You are a talented young woman."

The man started to move on. The ball of yarn in Fanny's lap rolled onto the carpet and across the room. The governor stooped to pick it up and as the yarn was rewound, talked to Fanny. Her plan had worked!

Fanny chuckled when she was alone. Her needles clicked as she knitted. *I'd like to meet other famous people, too, like senators and poets. I wonder who will be next to tour the school.*

At an evening party sometime later Fanny's wish came true. America's well-known poet, William Bryant, visited. Shaking her hand, he said, "Miss Crosby, I am aware of your poetry. I've read several poems by the 'Blind Poetess.' You have great talent. You must continue writing."

Encouragement like that strengthened Fanny for the hot summer months ahead. Together with other students from the school, Fanny traveled by canal boat through New York. In little towns along the way the group sang and recited to show what blind people could learn.

"Oswego! Next stop–Os-we-go!" The students got ready to leave the boat.

"I hope something good comes out of this trip," Fanny murmured as she left the boat for the hall. She overheard whispers of the townspeople as she waited for the program to begin.

"Which one is the 'Blind Poetess'?" "Think she'll give a poem tonight?" "Better be a good one!"

Show Illustration #11

When it was her turn, Fanny quoted one of her long poems and played the piano and harp. When the meeting was over a mother introduced her son. "After hearing you and the other students tonight, I know the Institute for the Blind is the best place for Van," she told Fanny. "He'll be coming to the school as soon as I can arrange it. Will you please take care of him?" Fanny assured the mother she would.

It had been a tiring trip and Fanny looked forward to returning to school. In the fall she would be a teacher! On the way home, she rested. The water slapped gently against the barge. The creaks of the boat reminded her of the trip she'd taken years before when she was a child. That had been a sad trip when she had learned she would never see.

So much has happened since then, Fanny thought. *I've learned a lot. I've met many important people. I wonder what Grandmother would think now. She always said God had a special plan for me. Of course, I haven't thought too much about God. I've been so busy.*

Show Illustration #1

Memorizing those Bible verses at Grandma's knee seemed like a long time ago. Any thoughts of God and His plan for the rest of her life were pushed aside. Fanny had to concentrate on preparing lessons for her classes. But down in her heart Fanny didn't feel right about trying to put thoughts of God out of her mind.

Back at school, Fanny studied and taught all day and evening. Then she stayed up until one or two o'clock in the morning composing poems. She had been invited to recite before members of the Congress and wanted to do well. Friends encouraged her to publish a book of poetry. By winter she was exhausted and had to see the school doctor.

"Fanny, I'm afraid you'll have to give up teaching until you are stronger," the doctor said. "In fact, I think you should not go to Washington, DC."

"Oh, no, Doctor!" Fanny cried. "I'll give up teaching for a while. But I must go to Washington! I've looked forward to this trip."

The doctor was silent for what seemed like a long time. "Well, Fanny," he said at last. "If you don't go to Washington, you'll worry and become sicker. You may go. But don't over-do. Not everyone has the privilege of speaking before Congress."

In January, Fanny traveled with a group of the students to the nation's Capitol. Senators, representatives and people from the city crowded into the Assembly Hall.

Show Illustration #12

The Congressional Chamber was so quiet Fanny's voice was the only sound. When she ended her long poem, there was a hushed pause, then a tremendous burst of applause which frightened Fanny. She had forgotten how many people were there. The audience refused to stop clapping. Fanny was called back to recite again.

What shall I say? she thought wildly. Then she knew! Calmly, she quoted a poem she had written about the secretary of state who had died the previous summer.

A sister of the man about whom the poem was written was in the audience. She met Fanny afterward and slipped a ring on her finger. "This is to thank you for the lovely poem about my brother," she said gratefully.

The young people traveled back to New York. Fanny continued writing her poetry. She returned to teaching. From time to time she welcomed important visitors to the Institute.

One day another US president stopped at the school. After the program, President Polk invited Fanny to stroll about the grounds with him. Suddenly Fanny heard the voice of an elderly servant who had worked at the school.

"Excuse me, please, Mr. President. I must leave you for a moment." Fanny rushed down the path to greet her friend.

When she returned, Fanny apologized. Perhaps the president would think her rude for leaving him to talk to the old servant.

President Polk said kindly, "Fanny, I commend you. You left a president to greet a servant. I respect you for showing such kindness."

Presidents and servants, rich and poor, sighted and blind–Fanny had met many people. But she still hadn't met the most important person–the Lord Jesus Christ. Fanny was going her own way. She cared more about the praise people gave her than she did about knowing what God wanted her to do.

Then one day, something happened that made Fanny think about God again. A terrible disease called cholera began to spread through the country. Everyone was afraid it would reach New York City where Fanny lived. Many of the students had left the school for the blind to try to keep from getting sick.

> ## NOTE TO THE TEACHER
>
> Cholera is an infectious disease which usually causes death. People who have contacted cholera have diarrhea, vomiting and muscle cramps. Modern medicine prevents cholera epidemics today.

Fanny shivered as she walked through the school dorm. Everything was so quiet and still. The few students remaining at school had gone to bed. She sighed as she headed for her own room.

As she walked past the superintendent's office, she rapped lightly on the door before entering. "All is well, Sir. Good night," she called

"Fanny! Wait! Are you sure you should stay?" the superintendent asked. "It might not be safe."

"Sir, if the cholera epidemic does reach New York City, God can take care of us just as well here," she replied. "And we can be of some help."

"Yes, I suppose you are right. Well, good night."

How strange for me to talk of God only when I need Him, Fanny thought. *If Grandmother knew I've been too busy for God, she would be disappointed. It's been so long since she taught me about Him. One of her favorite verses was "Be strong and of a good courage, fear not, nor be afraid . . . for the Lord . . . will go with thee"* (Deuteronomy 31:6). *I need that verse now.*

Fanny entered her room and dressed for bed. "It seems right to talk about God now," she thought out loud. "So many people are sick and dying. How horrible death is!"

Every day newspapers reported how the epidemic spread. People talked of nothing else. Seventy thousand people had died in England from the dreaded disease. Now cholera had come to the United Stares. In New Orleans, more than 3,000 died. In Philadelphia, thousands more were buried.

It was spring when cholera struck New York City. As many as 800 people were dying each week. Fanny was saddened when one and then another of the blind students became ill and died. "Oh, God, this epidemic must end soon," Fanny cried when she learned the tenth student had died.

Show Illustration #13

Fanny and the school doctor trudged daily to a nearby hospital. There they cared for the sick. Often Fanny spent hours making cholera pills for the patients. Every day special wagons rattled through the streets. The wagon masters called, "Bring out your dead. Bring out your dead."

Fanny shuddered every time she heard those words. *It's frightening enough to stumble over coffins in the halls,* she thought as she walked to another room.

She leaned wearily against the doorframe. Her stomach hurt. *Oh no!* Fanny thought fearfully. *I can't get sick! I must take some of the pills I've been making.* Returning to the Institute, she went to bed. *God will do what is best,* she reasoned. *If I get cholera, He will care for me.* Then she fell asleep.

What was going to happen to Fanny? Would she get cholera? We'll find out in our next chapter!

The *aim* of the chapter: To help students realize that God wants to save us from sin and to use our abilities to serve Him.

Fanny had been working hard to take care of the people who were sick with cholera. But then she started to feel sick herself! She went back to the Institute and crawled into bed. Soon she was asleep.

The next morning when Fanny awoke she was completely well. The superintendent and doctor who suspected Fanny might still be sick stopped her before she left for the hospital. "No, Fanny," they said. "You must leave New York. Go home and rest. We cannot lose one of our best teachers."

At home in Bridgeport, Connecticut, Fanny tried to rest. But she could not forget the sorrow and death she had felt in the city. She was restless and discouraged. *Where would I have gone if I had died?* she pondered. *I told Grandmother I would meet her in Heaven. Now I'm not sure I would go there. I'm afraid I lied to Grandmother.*

In the fall the epidemic was over and Fanny returned to the Institute. The once happy teacher was now sad as she taught her classes.

Fanny sat in her classroom alone one afternoon. When footsteps stopped outside the door, she turned her head expecting a student to ask help with the lesson she had assigned.

Show Illustration #14

Instead, one of the teachers said, "Fanny, we've a few minutes before going to supper. May I speak with you?"

"Why, yes, Mr. Camp," Fanny exclaimed in surprise.

"Fanny, the Broadway Tabernacle on 30th Street is having revival meetings. You've been so discouraged since the epidemic. I thought perhaps something might be said there that would encourage you. I am going down tonight. Will you go with me?"

"Perhaps sometime I'll go, Mr. Camp," Fanny replied. "But not tonight, though I appreciate your asking me."

Later in the evening Fanny listened to the rain ping against the window in her room. *Why was I afraid to go with Mr. Camp to the meeting tonight?* she wondered. *Is it because I'm trying to hold onto God with one hand and what I want with the other hand? I guess I've become proud of being called the "Blind Poetess." I've wanted to meet famous and important people more than obey God. I'm not really a Christian.*

That night Fanny dreamed Mr. Camp was dying. Standing by his bed she heard him ask, "Fanny, will you meet me in Heaven?"

"Yes, I will, God helping me," Fanny promised.

"Remember, you promised a dying man," Mr. Camp whispered as the dream ended.

"Will you meet me in Heaven?" The question bothered Fanny for several days. She knew the answer was "no."

I do believe in God, Fanny said to herself. *I know He loves me. I've even prayed many times. Why do I still feel like I'm carrying a heavy burden?*

Mr. Camp asked Fanny again to attend the revival meetings. This time she said "yes." She listened carefully to the sermon. Then the congregation sang a hymn.

At the cross, at the cross
Where I first saw the light,
And the burden of my heart rolled away.
It was there by faith I received my sight,
And now I am happy all the day.

Fanny understood why she felt as she did. *The song tells of Jesus who died on the cross for my sin*, Fanny thought. *The burden I feel is because I have not believed He died for me. My sin has not been forgiven.*

As the song continued, Fanny realized, *Why, I can't do anything to get peace with God. God and Jesus have done it all for me. All I must do is believe and receive.*

That night Fanny believed Jesus died for her. She asked God to forgive her sin. The burden she felt was gone! She jumped to her feet and shouted, "Hallelujah!"

Show Illustration #15

As Fanny returned to the Institute after the meeting she thought, *Now I know I'll meet Grandmother someday. I'm not afraid to die. I know I'm going to Heaven.*

A week later Fanny went to a Bible class. She listened as men and women told when they believed and received Jesus as Saviour. Before, Fanny had always asked not to be called on to give a testimony. Now she wanted to! Eagerly she stood and told what happened at the revival meeting. As she sat down she thought, *That was well said.*

"Fanny," a little voice inside seemed to say, "you still have a problem with pride. Are you sure you really received Christ as your Saviour? If you did, you probably wouldn't have felt so satisfied with what you said just now."

The joy Fanny had felt was gone. She didn't realize her enemy, Satan, would bring things to her mind that would cause her to doubt. She asked a friend, "Am I truly a Christian?"

(*Teacher:* Print Fanny's question on a flash card: "Am I truly a Christian?" Show flash card here and use it for the invitation at conclusion of chapter.)

"Oh, yes, Fanny," the friend assured her. "If you truly believe Jesus died for you, and asked God to forgive your sin, Christ is now your Saviour. God keeps His promises. He wouldn't trick you. Be sure to trust God instead of yourself. You might be holding back from trusting God all the way by thinking you can make your own decisions. Give everything to Him. He wants to be your Saviour and your Lord."

When Fanny told the Lord, "I surrender. I give You everything. I'll do anything and everything You ask me to do," the joy returned.

God heard what Fanny prayed. Now He could use her. Now Fanny was willing to follow God's plan, not her own.

What does God want me to do? Fanny wondered.

As Fanny waited for God to show her what she should do next, a new school term began at the Institute. Fanny stood in the open doorway listening to the children's laughter as they played on the lawn. Crunch! Someone was walking up the driveway. Sniff! Sniff-sniff! Someone was crying!

Fanny stepped outside and waited until the person came closer. "May I help you?" she asked gently.

A small voice said brokenly, "I want to go ... home." Sniff.

Show Illustration #16

Fanny reached out and pulled the young child to her. "Why do you want to go home, Sarah?" she asked, wiping away the tears.

"Everything is so … diff'rent and … and scary," Sarah stammered. "I'm afraid."

"Why, Sarah," Fanny said, "that's exactly what I thought when I came to the Institute. And I was much older than you are! But then I made friends. Would you like to hear about my first days here?"

Fanny felt the little girl nod her head. Taking her by the hand, she led Sarah inside where all was quiet and they could be alone. Soon Sarah's crying stopped. She even giggled.

"Oh, I like you, Miss Crosby," she exclaimed, throwing her arms around Fanny's neck.

Everyone liked Fanny, both students and teachers. Lonely students learned she was their friend. She listened to their problems and cheered those who were discouraged. Even teachers at the Institute asked Fanny for help.

One day Fanny heard the music teacher playing a tune on the piano.

"Why, Mr. Root, how wonderful! You should publish that!" Fanny exclaimed.

"I have no words for the song, Fanny, just the tune," George Root replied.

"This is what your melody says to me," Fanny said and quoted a poem she had just thought of.

Mr. Root was pleased. Throughout the summer Fanny wrote several songs for the music teacher. Some became popular. The songs earned quite a bit of money for Mr. Root, but Fanny was paid only a few dollars.

However, Fanny received something better than money! She learned she could write poems for music which people enjoyed singing. It seemed God was showing her which direction to take. Knowing God's will was better than money.

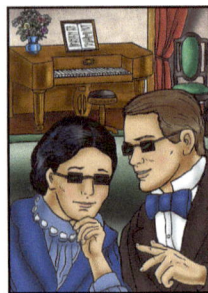

Show Illustration #17

At the same time Fanny was writing songs for George Root, another teacher was singing songs to Fanny–love songs! Fanny had met him years before when the students from the Institute were on a boat trip. His mother had introduced them and told Fanny he would be going to the Institute for the Blind.

Alexander Van Alstyne, or Van as he was called, had attended the Institute, graduated and then went to college. Now he played the piano, organ and trumpet; composed songs; and taught music. He returned to the Institute as a teacher.

Van and Fanny were both musicians. He wrote music and she wrote poems. Van discovered that the words of the love songs he sang to Fanny said what he felt for her.

"Fanny," Van began one evening, "I love you. I would like you to be my wife. But would you want a blind man for your husband?"

"If you want a blind woman for your wife, I can want a blind man for my husband," Fanny replied with a laugh. "I love you, too, Van. Yes, I want to be your wife."

Soon after that, Van left the Institute and became a private music teacher. Several months later, Fanny resigned her teaching position and also left the school. She traveled to the small New York town where Van lived. There they were married.

Fanny was now a blind housewife. Few of her neighbors knew she was a well-known poet writing her third book. She was happy with her kind, cheerful husband. Van was not only kind to Fanny, he gave music lessons to the poor children in town and charged them very little. He supported Fanny by playing the organ in several churches. Their first year together went by quickly.

It was an exciting day when Fanny knew she was to become a mother. Van and Fanny waited eagerly. But when the baby was born, it did not live. Fanny said later, "The angels came down and took our child up to God and His throne." She would not talk about the child. She was very sad.

As the days passed, Fanny remembered one of Grandmother's favorite verses: "The eternal God is thy refuge, and underneath are the everlasting arms." Over and over Fanny prayed, "My baby's death seems more than I can bear. But thank You, Father, for Your comfort."

The next year Fanny and Van moved back to New York City. Soon afterward the Civil War began and Fanny wrote patriotic and war songs. But there were more important songs to be written.

The churches needed hymns and gospel songs–songs people would enjoy singing, songs which would encourage Christians to obey the Lord.

William Bradbury was a man who had been writing hymns since the beginning of the great revival. His melodies were loved by the people who sang them.

But he wanted new poems set to music. He was delighted when a minister told him he was sending a lady who could write the poems he needed. He was especially delighted when he heard the lady was the "Blind Poetess," Fanny Crosby.

Fanny was just as excited about her appointment with Mr. Bradbury. God assured her this was an important meeting. It was as if He said to her: "This is it, Fanny. You are going to be a hymn writer."

Show Illustration #18

"Fanny," Mr. Bradbury said when introduced to her, "I thank God that we have met at last. I believe you can write hymns. I have wished for a long time to have a talk with you."

He sent her home with an assignment. Fanny was to return within a week with a hymn that would show Mr. Bradbury whether or not she could write hymns. What a challenge!

Ever since the death of her baby, Fanny had been discouraged. Now as she remembered the Scriptures she had memorized as a child, the words for the song began to come.

"I shall write of Heaven and how beautiful it is," she declared. "Someday I shall go there. How sunshiny it will be! I shall see Jesus–and my little baby. We shall never be separated again."

Fanny smiled. The sadness she had felt seemed to be going away as she composed the hymn.

Three days later Fanny was back in the office with her first hymn. She waited while Mr. Bradbury looked at her poem. He stroked his bushy beard as he read it.

The song was perfect! It had everything Mr. Bradbury wanted. "Fanny, I will use this in the hymnbook I'm preparing now," he said warmly.

The next week, Mr. Bradbury called Fanny to come quickly to his office. He had a tune for a song, but he needed words desperately. He played the melody several times. Fanny listened carefully until she had the rhythm and melody memorized. Within a day she was back with several stanzas.

When Mr. Bradbury read the words, he said, "Fanny, I am surprised beyond measure. Let me say that as long as I have a publishing house, you will always have work."

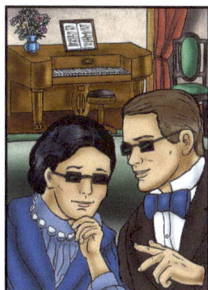

Show Illustration #17

That evening Fanny shared the good news with her husband. "Van, God has done so much for me. He allowed me to go to school when I wanted to so very much. I learned to write poetry and teach at the Institute. And best of all, I received the Lord as my Saviour. God was so patient with me. He brought us together, too. And then He took our little baby to Heaven. I don't know why He did that. But God is good. He does not make mistakes. Now I feel the most important part of my life is just beginning."

Fanny was ready to do what God had planned.

Now Fanny visited Mr. Bradbury's office regularly. Sometimes Mr. Bradbury assigned her a title or subject for a song. Often he played a tune for which Fanny was to write words. And sometimes she brought in songs she had composed on her own.

One day, Fanny stood on the sidewalk in front of the office for W. B. Bradbury & Co. A strong gust of wind swept down the street. She listened to the leaves scratch the sidewalk as the wind carried them along. Straightening her hat, she climbed the steps to the door wondering, *Will Mr. Bradbury like my newest hymn?*

Show Illustration #18

"Fanny," Mr. Bradbury exclaimed after he had heard the poem, "how do you write such perfect songs? They are just what the churches need!"

The little woman leaned forward, "Why, Sir, I always pray before thinking of even one word. God gives me the ideas. He helps me remember Scripture verses I've memorized. And He guides me to choose the right words."

Mr. Bradbury was not well and often had to go away for a rest. Finally he became so sick that he could not set Fanny's songs to music. He called for Fanny. "This is my final interview," he said. "My work is done. You must continue what I have begun. I am going to be forever with the Lord."

Four years after they met, Mr. Bradbury died and Fanny was heartbroken. The first hymn they had composed together was sung at the funeral. At the end of the service she felt God say to her, "Fanny, pick up the work where William Bradbury left it."

But this would be a very big job. Will Fanny be able to do it? You'll have to find out in our next chapter!

Chapter 5

The *aim* of the chapter: That students would determine to faithfully serve God in every opportunity He gives.

Fanny and Mr. Bradbury had worked together writing songs for four years, but now Mr. Bradbury had died. Fanny was sure that God wanted her to go on doing this work.

So Fanny continued working for their publishing company. Soon she was their most well-known songwriter. Because of the growing popularity of her hymns, she was invited to speak at YMCA's, missions, churches and prisons.

A friend felt Fanny needed someone else to set her hymns to music and urged her to send her latest poem to Howard Doane.

Howard Doane was a rich businessman who had written music since he was 16. He was only 30 when he had a heart attack. While recovering from his illness, he felt God wanted him to write sacred melodies and compile hymnbooks. But Mr. Doane was not a poet and some of his best tunes had no words.

While on a visit to New York City he was asked to write a hymn for the anniversary of a mission. He had a tune in mind but no poem could be found. Kneeling on the floor of his hotel room, he asked God to send him a suitable poem and a poet who could write words for all of his songs.

Show Illustration #19

Just then, someone knocked on the door. A messenger boy handed him an envelope addressed to Mr. William Howard Doane. Quickly he read the letter.

"Mr. Doane, I have never met you, but I feel impelled to send you this hymn. May God bless it. Fanny Crosby."

The poem began: "More like Jesus would I be ..." It said just what Doane wanted. He sat down and wrote a gentle tune for the words.

When the mission director heard the song he exclaimed, "Oh, where did you get that song?"

Mr. Doane answered, "Fanny Crosby sent it. Do you know where I can find her?" Writing down her address, Howard Doane determined to meet her. Wealthy, well-dressed Howard Doane felt people staring at him as he climbed to the third floor of the poor tenement house one evening. He knocked at the attic door to which he had been directed. A little woman answered the door and peered at Mr. Doane through greenish colored glasses.

"Could you please direct me to Miss Fanny Crosby?" he asked.

Fanny smiled. "I am Fanny. Welcome to my home."

Show Illustration #20

Mr. Doane was shocked at her surroundings. But he was even more shocked to learn Fanny could not see him through her glasses.

Putting Mr. Doane at ease, Fanny said, "God bless you, dear friend! How glad I am to find you!"

Mr. Doane pressed a bill into Fanny's hand. "This is for the song you sent me," he said as he urged her to keep the money.

Fanny thought the payment was the usual dollar or two she received for a song. Later someone told her it was a $20 bill! Mr. Doane intended to pay her well.

As the weeks passed, Fanny enjoyed working with Mr. Doane. He introduced her to his wife, whose name was also Fanny. Soon she felt like a member of their family.

Show Illustration #21

Fanny continued to speak to different groups. In one prison a man realized he was a sinner and called out, "Good Lord, do not pass me by!" At home that evening Fanny wrote the words for the song "Pass Me Not, O Gentle Saviour." Howard Doane wrote the music. When it was sung in the prison, several prisoners were saved.

After a while the song was used in revival meetings and churches throughout the world. As Fanny traveled around the country, people told her how the song led them to accept Christ as their Saviour.

Show Illustration #20

One day Mr. Doane rushed into Fanny's apartment. "Fanny, I have exactly 40 minutes to catch my train to a Sunday school convention. Here is a tune. See if it says anything to you." He hummed the simple melody once.

Fanny clapped her hands. "Why, that says, 'Safe in the Arms of Jesus,'" She hurried to the other room in her apartment, knelt and prayed. In a half hour she returned and dictated three stanzas and a chorus.

Mr. Doane introduced the song at the Sunday school convention. It became a favorite immediately. Eventually it was translated into over 200 languages. For the rest of her life Fanny received letters about this song from all parts of the world. Christians who were dying were comforted by the song. A prisoner continued to believe by repeating the words constantly. A sailor on the high seas was saved when he heard the song.

By this time Fanny had written many hymns. Her songs appeared in dozens of hymnbooks. And because some publishers wanted different authors' names in their books, Fanny used over 200 pen names (Pen names are made-up names which writers may use instead of their own. This is not considered dishonest, so it was all right for Fanny to do this.)

Fanny learned that even people in England were singing her songs. The American evangelist, Dwight L. Moody, and his song leader, Ira Sankey, were holding meetings in that country. Many were saved as they listened to "Pass Me Not, O Gentle Saviour." She was thrilled to know that God was using her hymns across the ocean.

But Fanny was not getting rich through her writing. Fanny and Van had chosen to live in the poorer sections of New York City so they could help their neighbors. Much of the money Fanny received from her songs was given away. One day when it was time to pay the rent, there was not enough money. Fanny wondered how they would pay their apartment rent. She decided to pray and ask God to supply the money. Shortly after she prayed, a man stopped Fanny as she walked down the street, pressed a $10 bill into her hand and left. The rent could be paid! The bill was exactly what was needed.

That night Fanny wrote the song, "All the Way My Saviour Leads Me." The words told of God's faithfulness in meeting her need.

The next year the evangelistic team, Moody and Sankey, came to America. Fanny met them in New York. They used her songs in every meeting. Fanny was on her way to reaching the greatest goal of her life–having one million people won to Christ through her hymns.

Fanny's hymns could win a person to Christ because they were so filled with Scripture. But Fanny herself also led many people to the Saviour. God was using her now as He had planned. And God had other plans for Fanny's life.

One day, Fanny stood at the window of her little home, listening to the clatter of horses' hooves against the street and the rattle of wagons as they came and went. Fanny listened to shouts and laughing voices of children echoing between the apartment buildings. She smiled as she thought of the parties she had planned for her neighbors over the years. The parents had enjoyed the entertainment as much as their children.

While some felt it was a waste of time to plan these parties, Fanny delighted in making others happy. She tried to help them forget their poor surroundings. Her love for the Lord Jesus made people want to know Him too.

"If only I were home more often," Fanny said to herself. "Then I could help my neighbors when they face problems."

Show Illustration #21

Fanny was a popular speaker. She traveled long distances alone to tell others of the Lord Jesus Christ. When she was home she went down into New York City's worst area to work in a mission several days a week. She listened to the men and women. She talked about how the Lord Jesus could help them. She prayed for those who attended the services. And she led many to receive the Lord Jesus as Saviour. After working 25 years in the mission, she said about the men who smelled bad and lived in terrible conditions, "Not one was ever ugly to me. They were my boys and I loved them all."

Show Illustration #22

After long, busy days, Fanny wrote songs late into the night. While others slept, the little, bent-over woman composed poems and prayed. She prayed for all who visited her during the day. She prayed for the pastors and churches in the city. And she prayed for the United States and its president.

The "Blind Poetess," who had met many presidents, was now known around the world as the "Queen of Gospel Songwriters." Fanny didn't like either title. She declared over and over to her friends, "I am doing what I can with what God has given me. More than anything, I desire that the hymns I write will bring people to Christ." Fanny's songs were doing that. She had written nearly 8,000 songs, and thousands of people had been saved.

Writing. Traveling. Speaking. "Fanny, you're doing too much!" her friends cautioned. "Nothing but death can make me stop my work for Christ," she answered. After her eightieth birthday, she became ill with pneumonia and friends thought she would not live. But she did live, and this time she followed the advice of her family. She left New York City and moved to Bridgeport, Connecticut, to live with her sister, where she could rest.

Van, who was also sick, was being cared for by friends. He died months after Fanny recovered from her illness. Fanny was heartbroken. But she determined, even in her sorrow, to keep busy. More hymns were written.

Fanny continued to speak wherever she was invited. She no longer traveled alone. She had a traveling companion on all her journeys. Because she was so lively, she wore out her companions even though they were younger. The women had to take turns traveling with Fanny with time off between trips.

Wherever Fanny went she told others about the Lord Jesus. Sometimes she told when she believed and received the Lord Jesus as her Saviour and Lord. Other times she spoke about prayer: "I pray for little needs and big needs. Sometimes God does not give me what I request. Then I know He has something better for me."

Often Fanny had a speaking engagement every day of the week, and sometimes several times a day. Thursdays, however, when she lived in Bridgeport, she had open house for anyone who wanted or needed to come see her. She never turned away a person who needed help.

One man said to her, "If only I were rich, all my problems would be solved."

Fanny smiled, "No, you would just have new problems," she said. "As for me, take the world, but give me Jesus." That night she wrote another hymn and called it "Take the World But Give Me Jesus."

Show Illustration #23

Children in Bridgeport enjoyed visiting "Aunt Fanny." She was invited to go with them to a party in the park. There, with the children around her, Fanny used a book of colors to tell them about the Lord Jesus.

She started at the back page of the book. "This gold page," she said, "reminds us of Heaven. God is in Heaven and He wants us to live there with Him someday. Heaven is a perfect place. There is no sickness, or sadness, or sin there and never will be." Fanny then turned to the first page. "This dark page can remind us of sin, because the Bible says that 'men loved darkness rather than light because their deeds were evil' (John 3:19). Evil means sin. God's Word often speaks of sin as darkness. The Bible says, 'All have sinned . . .' Children, if there is no sin in Heaven, and everyone has sinned, how can we go to Heaven? Our sin must be taken away. Only God could solve that problem, and He did.

"God loves us and wants us in Heaven with Him. So He made a way for us to go to Heaven. God said that sin must be punished and the punishment for sin is death. God sent His Son, the Lord Jesus Christ, to earth. The Lord Jesus never sinned. He lived a perfect life. But wicked men hated Him and killed Him. The Bible says 'Christ died for *our* sins' (1 Corinthians 15:3). Jesus was punished instead of us when He died on the cross. This red page reminds me of the blood of the Lord Jesus which flowed from His body when He died. But, He did not stay dead. Three days after Jesus died, He came alive. He is living in Heaven today.

"If you believe Jesus, God's Son, died on the cross for you, and if you ask Him to forgive your sin, He will forgive you. You will be made clean like this white page. God will look at you as if you had not sinned. Then someday you will go to Heaven."

Show Illustration #24

One thing the children loved about Fanny was her cheerfulness. And that cheerfulness never left her. When a reporter was interviewing her at age 92, she said to him, "When you publish that I am 92, make that 92 years young! I feel young. I am the happiest person alive. If you should know anyone who is any happier, bring him to me. I want to shake his hand." She had lived a long life, she said, because she had learned through prayer to control her appetite, her temper and her tongue. "I try never to think an unkind thought about another person and never say an unkind word to anyone," Fanny explained.

There were many honors for Fanny during the last 20 years of her life. Birthday parties, national celebrations, banquets in her honor. Once a band escorted her to a meeting playing one of her songs as they walked through the streets.

Fanny was alarmed when she learned many people no longer believed all of the Bible. Some said it was full of fairy tales. She declared firmly, "The Bible is God's word! All of it! My love for the Bible is stronger now than when I was young. This book is God's treasure house. It is the lantern that lights my pathway Home."

On an evening in February when Fanny was 94 years old, she said to some friends, "I don't feel well tonight. But tomorrow I shall be better," she added happily. At nine o'clock that night (February 11, 1915) she sent for her secretary and asked her to write a letter to a neighbor family whose child had just died. She assured them, "Your precious Ruth is 'Safe in the Arms of Jesus.'" Then she dictated a poem she had written during the day.

Fanny Crosby died that night. She had fulfilled her wish to serve Christ even on her last day on earth. She had given everything she had to her Saviour. And even today He is receiving the honor as her songs are still being sung in churches around the world!

Review Questions for *Fanny Crosby, the Blind Poet*
by Hannah Landis

Chapter 1

1. What story did Fanny want her grandmother to tell her? *(The story of why she couldn't see)*
2. What had happened to Fanny when she was a baby that caused her to become blind? *(A doctor tried to help her when she was sick, but he hurt her eyes.)*
3. Fanny was waiting for someone to come home from school and play with her—who was it? *(Her aunt Polly)*

4. When Polly got home from school, what did Fanny tell her she wanted to do someday? *(Go to school too)*
5. Fanny could do lots of things, even though she couldn't see. What were some of the things she could do? *(Run without bumping into things, dress and eat by herself, hear very well, smell flowers, etc.)*
6. What special book did Grandmother read to Fanny? *(The Bible)*

7. Can you remember one of the things Grandmother told Fanny about God? *(God never sins; God must punish sin; God is loving; God sent Jesus; God wants us to know Him.)*
8. Fanny's mother Mercy had a plan to help Fanny—what was it? *(To take her to see a famous doctor in the city)*
9. What did Mercy hope that the doctor could do for Fanny? *(Operate on her eyes so she could see)*
10. At first, was Fanny excited about the plan? *(Yes)*

Chapter 2

1. What sad thing did Dr. Mott tell Fanny about her eyes? *(She would never be able to see.)*
2. When Fanny was eight years old, she wrote a poem and showed it to her Grandmother—what was the poem about? *(Being blind)*
3. What did Grandmother and Mrs. Hawley help Fanny to memorize? *(Entire books of the Bible)*
4. When Mrs. Hawley asked Fanny if she had cut her white rose, what did Fanny say? *(She lied and said "no.")*
5. What did Fanny and Grandmother pray about? *(They asked God to make a way for Fanny to go to school.)*
6. What did Fanny say when Grandmother asked her if she would meet her in Heaven someday? *(She said yes, but only to make her Grandmother feel better.)*
7. What exciting news did Fanny's mother tell her? *(She could attend the Institute for the Blind.)*
8. How did Fanny feel about the institute when she first got there? *(She was lonely and homesick.)*
9. What wrong thing did Fanny and her friend Jean do? *(Stole a watermelon)*
10. Fanny learned to do lots of things at the institute, but there was one thing she liked best and was very good at—what was it? *(Writing poems)*

Chapter 3

1. What rule did Dr. Jones make about Fanny's poems? *(She could not write any poems for three months.)*
2. What happened to Fanny when she couldn't write poems? *(She couldn't concentrate on her schoolwork and started to get bad grades.)*
3. What did Dr. Jones do when he saw how much Fanny needed to write poems? *(He let her write poems again, and even had her study with a writing teacher.)*
4. How did Fanny feel about the important people who came to the school for the blind? *(She wanted to meet them and talk to them.)*
5. As Fanny traveled with the other students from the institute, she met a mother and her son. After seeing what Fanny had learned at the institute, what did the mother decide to do? *(Send her blind son to the institute as well)*
6. What new job did Fanny start when she came back from her trip? *(She became a teacher at the institute.)*
7. The Congressmen in Washington, DC, liked Fanny's poem so much, what did they do? *(They called her back to recite another poem.)*
8. Fanny met many people–even the president! But what most important Person had she not yet met? *(The Lord*

Jesus)
9. Why were many of the students leaving the institute? *(Because they were afraid of getting sick with cholera)*
10. Every day Fanny was busy helping to take care of the sick, but what happened to Fanny at the very end of the story? *(She felt sick herself.)*

Chapter 4

1. What did Fanny keep thinking about that made her so sad and discouraged? *(Death; where she would go if she died)*
2. Where did Mr. Camp invite Fanny to go with him? *(To a special revival meeting)*
3. When Fanny finally agreed to go to the meeting, what happened to her there? *(She realized Jesus had died for her sins and believed in Him as her Saviour.)*
4. Later Fanny made another important decision. Whose plan for her life was she going to follow? *(God's)*
5. When Fanny heard Mr. Root playing music that had no words, what did she do? *(She made up a poem to be the words of the song)*
6. What did Fanny say when Van asked her to marry him? *(Yes)*
7. What sad thing happened to Fanny's baby? *(It died.)*
8. Mr. Bradbury wanted to see if Fanny could write words for the Christian songs he wrote. After reading her poems, what did he decide? *(That Fanny could always have a job writing lyrics for his music)*
9. How did Fanny get such good ideas for her songs? *(She prayed; she used the Bible verses she had memorized.)*
10. After Mr. Bradbury died, what did Fanny feel like God was telling her to do? *(Continue Mr. Bradbury's work as a hymn writer)*

Chapter 5

1. As Mr. Doane was praying and asking God to send him words for his music, what arrived for him in the mail? *(A poem from Fanny)*
2. Why was Mr. Doane surprised when he visited Fanny? *(She lived in such a small house; she could not see.)*
3. Fanny wrote many hymns with Mr. Doane and made a lot of money. What did Fanny do with her money? *(She gave most of it away to those who were poor.)*
4. What did Fanny want her hymns to do for others? *(Teach them about how Jesus could be their Saviour)*
5. Fanny did more than write hymns. Can you name some things Fanny did for others? *(Had parties for her neighbor children; traveled and spoke; mission work; prayed)*
6. While Fanny was resting after being sick, what happened to her husband Van? *(He died)*
7. Why did the young women who helped Fanny have to take turns traveling with her? *(Because she wore them out even though they were younger)*
8. Fanny loved to teach children using a book of colors. Can you remember what the colors remind us of? *(Gold–Heaven; dark–sin; red–Jesus' blood; white–forgiveness)*
9. When Fanny was 92 years old, what did Fanny say about herself? *(She felt young; was the happiest person alive)*
10. When did Fanny write her last poem? *(The day she died)*